unlimited theatre in association with **sheffield theatres** presents

safety
by chris thorpe

First performed at the **Traverse Theatre** in Edinburgh 1st August 2002

Michael: Steven Dykes
Tanya: Louisa Ashley
Susan: Bridget Escolme
Sean: Chris Thorpe

Directed by Jon Spooner

Stage Design: Barney George
Lighting Design: Tim Skelly
Assistant Lighting Designer: Chris Luffingham
Video/Projection: William Rose
Original Sound/Music: Chris Goode
Technical Support: Lee Dalley/Sarah Buckmaster
Company Manager: Liz Margree
Graphic Design: Andy Edwards
PR: Alex Gammie at Guy Chapman Associates

Presented in association with Sheffield Theatres

SAFETY is not an anti-news play. In a world increasingly lacking barriers to the transmission of informmation, events of political and human importance need to be covered more – and more effectively – if they are to stand out from the constant background roar of meaningless factoids that constitute the bulk of news reporting. Anyone who struggles, often at great personal risk, to illustrate the conflicts that we all part own as global citizens is doing an admirable and necessary job, for which some pay with their lives Images of suffering, both during conflict and in its

aftermath, have taken on iconic status however and as is the case with icons, have inevitably become commodified. The rise of war reporting as an industrial process has placed great strain on those who, often from the most altruistic of motives, have taken it upon themselves to witness human brutality and struggle first hand and pass those experiences on to the world. Sometimes proximity to inhumanity requires a surrendering of one's own humanity in the long term. It is this process that SAFETY sets out to investigate.

Chris Thorpe 2002

Steven Dykes is a founder member of NXT with whom he has toured throughout the UK, Europe and the USA, in premieres of plays by David Mamet, Heiner Muller, Enzo Cormann and David Bown. Other work includes roles with: Howard Barker's The Wrestling School, The Theatre Exchange (Minneapolis) and Theater M (New York).

Andy Edwards is a graphic designer/artist based in Leeds. He works in collaboration with a range of performers, artists and writers, and is exhibiting in a group show, The War Effort, at The Foundry, London.

Bridget Escolme is a lecturer in Theatre Studies at the University of Leeds where she teaches early modern drama in performance and contemporary performance practice. This is her second production with Unlimited Theatre, for whom she also played the role of Woman in STATIC.

Barney George has been designing for theatre since 1994. Recent projects include design for an adaptation by Mike Kenny of 'The Winter's Tale' for Interplay Theatre, directed by Steve Byrne and production design for 'Pericles' at The National Studio directed by Tassos Stevens. This is his first collaboration with Unlimited Theatre.

Chris Goode is the artistic director of Camden People's Theatre. His work is a musician and sound artist has included the duo COAT with Jeremy Hardingham. As a performance maker and writer he is best known for his work with Signal to Noise, including the solo show KISS OF LIFE at the Pleasance 2002; he also collaborated with Unlimited on the making of NEUTRINO.

Chris Luffingham is a freelance lighting designer. Winner of Best Lighting Design at the 2001 Student Drama Festival, Chris works with companies including Scottish Dance Theatre and Bristol-based Theatre of the Mind.

William Rose is an artist working with video projection and digital video technologies. He is co-curator of EVOLUTION, the experimental time-based arts strand of the Leeds International Film Festival and programme co-ordinator at LUMEN, a Leeds based digital arts agency.

Tim Skelly is a designer in residence at the Workshop Theatre, Leeds University. He has worked regularly with Unlimited Theatre, designing lighting most recently for NEUTRINO. Other recent lighting design work includes HIGH LAND and DADDY I'M NOT WELL for Scottish Dance Theatre, HIJRA for West Yorkshire Playhouse, TOSCA and NABUCCO for the Moldovan National Opera, and BROTHER JACQUES for Plymouth Theatre Royal.

The five permanent members of UNLIMITED THEATRE are Louisa Ashley, Clare Duffy, Liz Margree, Jon Spooner and Chris Thorpe. Based in Leeds UK, they have been working together since 1997 to make new theatre that offers a genuine alternative to the mainstream whilst also retaining a wide appeal.

If UNLIMITED were a band they would most like to be Fugazi (We stick to our vision, we operate as a unit, we retain our independence, we work hard without being po-faced and we rock. We are intense.) Or ABBA. For the same reasons.

If UNLIMITED could teach the world to sing they would teach it God Only Knows by The Beach Boys, Holiday in Cambodia by The Dead Kennedys, Fat Bottomed Girls by Queen and Are We Clever Or Are We Stupid? by Louisa.

unlimited theatre

SAFETY is the ninth new production that the Company has produced since its inception. It is the second in a planned trilogy of plays (of which STATIC was the first) written in response to the media's role in reporting violent political conflict. The third, provisionally titled DISNEYLAND (subject to Mickey Mouse's approval) is due for production sometime in 2003.

NEUTRINO (2001) and STATIC (2000) were both awarded Scotsman Fringe Firsts "for innovation in theatre and an outstanding production". STATIC was also recorded and broadcast on BBC Radio 4 and has toured internationally to Ireland, Zimbabwe and Germany and will visit The Philippines and Papua New Guinea in November 2002. Unlimited begin making a new company-devised show (working title COULD IT BE MAGIC?) in October 2003.

**Welcome to the shows.
We're glad you could make it.**

Join our email list to receive regular updates on where, when and what is Unlimited at
www.unlimited.org.uk

UNLIMITED THEATRE would like to acknowledge the support, encouragement and general beauty of the following: Paul Warwick, The Workshop Theatre at the University of Leeds, Annie Lloyd at LMU Studio Theatre, Simon Allen, Matthew Byam Shaw, Wendy Spon, Ed Collier, Unlimited Angels, Mairead Turner, Tom Sheils, Emma Unsworth, Gavin Macdonald, Joe Williams, John Donnelly, Jim Gitsham, Tim and Mark at Synergy, Dennis at Lumen, Spob, Delia and Jo, Paul Crewes and Stephen Snell at the West Yorkshire Playhouse, Interplay Theatre, everyone at Nick Hern Books, staff and crew at the Traverse Theatre, Yorkshire Arts, the Arts Council of England, the British Council, The Really Useful Group, The Charity of Thomas Wade, parents, families and loved ones.

This production is dedicated to the memory of Kitty Burrows who was too aware of the foibles of the world to pass up the good times when they came along.

contact

We genuinely appreciate and enjoy your feedback. If you want to pass on any thoughts, opinions or responses to any element of your Unlimited experience then please:

email us at feedback@unlimited.org.uk

or send us a postcard to:
Studio 11 Aire Street Workshops
30-34 Aire Street
Leeds LS1 4HT
UK

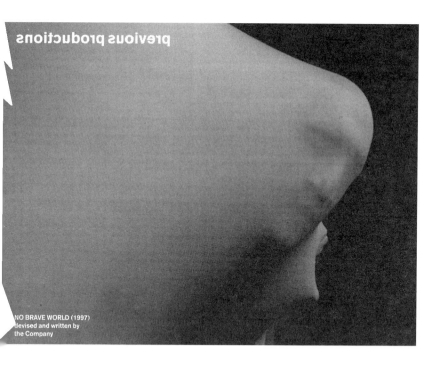

previous productions

NO BRAVE WORLD (1997)
devised and written by
the Company

THE SWING LEFT (2002) by Steven Dykes

THE SWING LEFT

CLEAN (2000) written by Clare Duffy

STATIC (1999) written by Chris Thorpe

WISE MAIDS (1997) written by Clare Duffy

NEUTRINO (2001) devised and written by the Company in collaboration with Chris Goode

WISE MAIDS

DEAD IN THE WATER (1999) written by Chris Thorpe

SHADES (1998) devised by the Company with text written by Clare Duffy

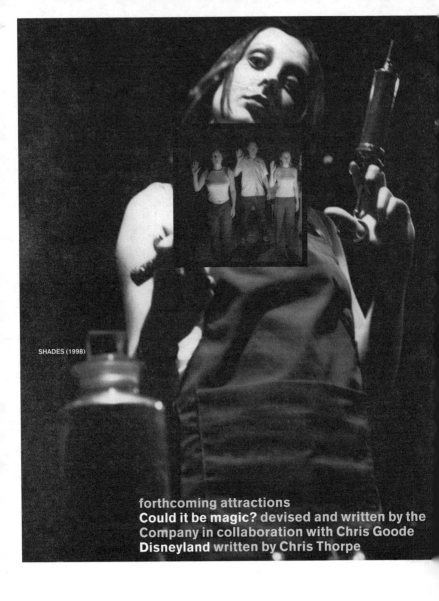

SHADES (1998)

forthcoming attractions
Could it be magic? devised and written by the Company in collaboration with Chris Goode
Disneyland written by Chris Thorpe

SAFETY

Chris Thorpe

in association with Unlimited Theatre

Notes on the text

A pause in speech is indicated thus . . .

A character being interrupted is indicated by a hyphen, thus –

Any specific directions for staging or the actors are marked in *italics*. It should be noted however that these directions are by no means prescriptive and will be influenced by subsequent development of the script, and decisions made by the director and designer both pre-production and in rehearsal.

This version of *Safety* was printed before the play's first performance and may have been modified slightly in the rehearsal process.

Characters

MICHAEL, *a photographer in his mid forties*
TANYA, *a reporter* (*late twenties/early thirties*)
SUSAN, *Michael's wife* (*late thirties/early forties*)
SEAN, *a young man in his late twenties*

Time
The present
1994

Settings
A hotel room, London
Michael and Susan's home, Northern England
The theatre, 'Michael's World'
A bombed-out house, somewhere in the Balkans, 1994

Scene One

A hotel room, London. Early afternoon.

A window, a desk (under the window), a chair, a wastebasket, a single bed (made up). On the desk is a neat pile of blank paper and a newspaper, half-read. There is a clean shirt casually thrown onto the bed.

MICHAEL, *shirtless. There is a towel around his neck and he is newly shaved. He is holding his hand to his jaw. He stands for a moment, looking blankly around the room. He takes his hand away from his jaw to examine it, revealing a small patch of blood.*

MICHAEL. Fuck it . . .

A passenger plane flies over at low altitude.

He wipes his hand on the towel, and then dabs the blood on his face away. Without looking where it lands, he tosses the towel away. He checks that his face has stopped bleeding, walks to the bed and pulls the shirt on. He sits on the bed, facing into the room, looking out of the window. Suddenly he moves to the desk and pulls it away from the window into another part of the room. He takes a packet of cigarettes from his trouser pocket and sits on the desk. He lights a cigarette, and looks around for an ashtray. Unable to find one, he folds one of the blank pieces of paper into a receptacle and taps his ash into it. He picks the newspaper up and glances at it, then drops it into the wastebasket. His mobile phone rings. He answers it.

MICHAEL. Hello?

. . .

Right. OK. Thanks.

MICHAEL *turns his phone off, goes and sits on the bed. He finishes his cigarette and stubs it out in the paper on the writing desk, then folds up the paper and drops it into the wastebasket. He looks out of the window. Another plane goes over. He shudders.* TANYA *enters. He has his back to her, and turns when she speaks, surprised.*

TANYA. Nice room.

. . .

MICHAEL. The paper said you'd be ten more minutes.

TANYA. I told them to.

MICHAEL. Wanted to catch me off guard?

TANYA. If you like.

MICHAEL. Staring pensively out of the window.

. . .

I assume that's told you something about me that you didn't already know?

TANYA. I thought you were just checking on your car.

. . .

Brightly.

So where do you want to do this?

MICHAEL. Well I thought since your paper went to the expense of booking me this lovely room, we could do it here. I'm not really in the mood for moving.

TANYA. It's a lovely day. Outside.

MICHAEL. It's a lovely day in London, outside. And I am fucking sick of London.

TANYA *removes a tape recorder from her bag and places it on the desk.*

TANYA. Well that's as interesting a place to start as any.

MICHAEL. What?

TANYA. 'I am fucking sick of London.' I like it. A nice, powerful opening line.

MICHAEL. Makes me sound like a whining bastard.

TANYA. It's expected of you. You're famous. In certain levels of society at least. People expect you to be a whining bastard. It fits their image of the way someone like you should be. The more disillusioned and bitter you seem, the more worth your photographs accrue.

TANYA *switches on the tape recorder.*

So. You're fucking sick of London, Michael. Why?

MICHAEL. Because nothing has ever happened to me here that wasn't to do with the simple mechanics of survival.

TANYA. That's a rather odd thing to hear. Coming from you.

MICHAEL. Why?

TANYA. The idea that you find London a difficult city to survive in. I would have thought, compared to your usual choice of working environment . . .

MICHAEL. I didn't say it was a difficult city to survive in. I said it was time consuming. Complex. Not particularly dangerous, I grant you, but complex all the same.

. . .

Listen. The areas of the world I normally work in, the options are narrower. You find a way to get where you are going. You go there. You do your job without getting shot, or stepping on a landmine, or taken hostage. And then you come back. You stay in what is normally the only place available, and you eat and drink whatever happens to be around on any particular day. Your choices are naturally limited. Compare that to the logistical nightmare that is, for example, travelling two miles in any direction in this fucking town, and trying to get a decent cup of coffee when you get there, and you can see why I hate the place.

. . .

There's too much interference. Too much shit between what you want to do and actually doing it. It's like living inside a detuned radio.

. . .

Say what you like about war. It's a fuck of a lot simpler.

TANYA. That's an interesting point – the simplicity of war. I've often thought, when looking at your photographs –

MICHAEL. Well that puts you a step ahead of most of your readers.

. . .

TANYA. I assume you want to be quoted on that?

MICHAEL. What do you think?

TANYA switches off the tape recorder.

TANYA. I think you're acting like a child.

MICHAEL. That's not a very professional thing to say.

TANYA. I think you and I broke the boundaries of professionalism a long time ago.

MICHAEL *laughs.*

MICHAEL. I suppose we did.

. . .

Are we going to break them again, today?

TANYA. That entirely depends on you giving me what I want.

MICHAEL. Which is?

TANYA. A series of straight answers to a series of straight questions.

MICHAEL. So you can give the readers what they want?

TANYA. Whatever. Just pretend to give a fuck. For a little while at least.

. . .

MICHAEL *reaches out and puts a hand on* TANYA*'s cheek.*

She removes it gently.

No.

MICHAEL *switches on the tape recorder.*

MICHAEL. Go on then. Shoot.

TANYA. Simplicity.

MICHAEL. For example.

TANYA. 'Dying teenage conscript, 1994.'

MICHAEL. . . .

Why that one?

TANYA. It's arguably your most famous photograph. Probably your most influential. It certainly won the most awards. And I think it shows the brutal simplicity of conflict better than any other.

MICHAEL. . . .

In what way?

TANYA. It's a boy, who doesn't understand fully where he is, and doesn't want to be there. He's lying in the road, alone, shot in the chest. He is looking into the camera, and he is going to die.

. . .

It doesn't get much simpler than that, surely?

MICHAEL. No. It doesn't.

. . .

MICHAEL*'s attitude changes.*

He is now very much aware of being interviewed.

I think when you record a moment like that, it gives the lie to the grander justifications bandied around for going to war, doesn't it? Politics, history, nationalism. All the big ideological sticks that are used to beat people into shape just reduce to simple issues, moment by moment, of survival or non-survival. Kill or be killed.

TANYA. And have recent events in your own life reinforced that view?

MICHAEL. I'm not sure I –

TANYA. Sorry. I'm referring to your daughter's recent accident.

MICHAEL. I'm not sure what that has to do with conflict as such. It was a swimming –

TANYA. I know. But still, as a father, to see your own child in mortal danger –

MICHAEL *switches the tape recorder off.*

MICHAEL. Where the fuck is this going?

TANYA. I'm asking about the mixing of your professional and personal life.

MICHAEL. My personal life has nothing to do with this.

TANYA. Even when you're fucking the interviewer?

MICHAEL. My daughter's accident has nothing to do with any war.

TANYA. Really? I think it bears striking similarities to your working situation.

. . .

TANYA *switches the tape recorder on.*

A child in peril. It's not exactly a new sight for you, is it? Some of your most affecting images are of children in danger. Pnomh Penh. Mogadishu. Vukovar. Pristina. Suppose what I'm asking is if there is any difference when it's your own child. In danger of drowning.

MICHAEL. Of course it is. But there are . . . yes, I'll grant you there are similarities.

TANYA. But fortunately she was saved, right?

MICHAEL. Yes. A young man, passing. He swam out to her and pulled her to the shore.

. . .

Something for which I'm obviously profoundly grateful.

TANYA. And have you met the young man in question?

MICHAEL. Not yet. I'm hoping to. Soon.

TANYA. But the central issue I'm getting at is if it changed your attitude to all those other children, when you were an observer at this . . . incident.

MICHAEL. Well I wouldn't say I was completely an observer. I saw Alice in the water, and as soon as I became aware of the reality of . . .

TANYA. The situation . . .

MICHAEL. Yes . . . He was in the water with her.

TANYA. Before you could get in yourself.

MICHAEL. He was closer.

. . .

He was a better swimmer.

TANYA. And you must have felt –

MICHAEL. Relief.

. . .

They look at each other for a long time.

That was all I felt.

MICHAEL *touches* TANYA*'s face again.*

She reaches out and stops the tape recorder.

She does not pull away from him.

Relief.

Blackout.

Scene Two

MICHAEL, *alone.*

MICHAEL. One of the first things you notice, coming under fire . . .

He laughs.

Christ. It sounds so fucking dramatic. It isn't. But one of the first things you notice, coming under fire is this – bullets don't make much noise. They hardly make a sound. Guns make a lot of noise, I grant you. A right bloody racket. But bullets *whisper*. Until they hit something. Then all that velocity, all that kinetic energy, gets transferred into pressure and heat. But still, it's not all that noisy.

. . .

First assignment I ever had, the man standing next to me got shot, and I didn't even notice. You must have heard the phrase so many times. 'One minute he was standing there, and the next, I turned around and he was gone'. As survivors' testimonies go it's almost a fucking cliché. But that's exactly what it was like. I turned my head to say something to him and he was lying on his back, choking to death. Shot right through the windpipe. He just looked up at me, tried to breathe a couple of times and then just gave up on living. Shut his eyes and died on me, right there on the floor. The main thing I remember was . . . annoyance. That his blood was on my shoes.

Blackout.

Scene Three

MICHAEL *and* SUSAN*'s house.*

SUSAN *is sitting at a table, working on a laptop. She is concentrating hard, with a couple of books open on the table in front of her.* MICHAEL *enters. He sits at the opposite end of the table. Long pause.*

MICHAEL. You forget, you know.

. . .

  SUSAN *continues to work while she speaks.*

SUSAN. Was that observation or imperative?

. . .

  It's just that there are a number of ways to interpret the statement you just made, Michael, and I'd hate to disappoint you by choosing the wrong one.

. . .

  Hmm?

. . .

  'You forget, you know?'

. . .

  See what I mean?

. . .

  Or rather, do I see what you mean? Is it a philosophical statement? Something about the inevitability of forgetting, the ultimate perishability of information, but also coupled with the permanence of a fundamental level of knowledge. So perhaps what you mean is '*Although* you forget *certain things, there are other things it is a given that* you know?'. Like breathing? Or how to fuck? No? Or that the processes of the losing and gaining of knowledge are interdependent. '*It is necessary that* you forget *in order that* you know?'

. . .

I like both of those very much. Whichever one you might mean. Both meanings reduce to an elegant equivalence. Don't they?

. . .

'You forget. You know.' It's almost . . . *oriental* in its simplicity. Very Zen.

. . .

Of course there's also a possible level of interpretation that's more directed. At me, personally. That it's an observation made by you that reflects a particular opinion or view of me.

. . .

That *I* forget. But yet also that *I* know.

. . .

Is that the sort of observation that a husband can reasonably make of his wife?

MICHAEL *takes out his cigarettes.*

Don't smoke in here. It makes me feel sick.

MICHAEL *puts the cigarettes away.*

I imagine it could be a compliment. On one level, that even after eight years of marriage, you are still discovering certain depths to me you hadn't before suspected . . . That suddenly it's occurred to you that I am a complex being who embodies certain philosophical principles with a hitherto unseen clarity. Of course that interpretation begs a few questions. What have I forgotten? For example. Of course if your observation's accurate, you're going to have to tell me that. By the very nature of forgetting, I can't inform you of what it actually is I've forgotten. Also, at the moment, I'm not sure to what you're referring when you say that I *know*. If that's what you mean. And are you expressing irritation at the things I've been so careless to forget, or approval of my innate knowledge of . . . what? *As* what? A wife? The mother of your child? As a translator,

I forget plenty. That's what dictionaries are for. But then how would you have a clue about how much I know in a professional capacity? You've never shown an interest. At least to my knowledge. Or maybe you did show an interest once and I've forgotten.

. . .

Or is it a command? *You* forget. *You* know. In which case you should be much more specific. You can't just ask me to forget everything. What do you want me to try and forget? Isn't it an unreasonable request? And as for what I know . . .

. . .

Well I know a lot of things.

. . .

I know a lot of things that you don't know I know. Or that you hope I don't know. It's difficult to tell. We don't often talk anymore do we? At least in person.

. . .

You forget. You know. You've forgotten many facts about me. Or facts you once knew about me. Or about the way you were with me.

. . .

However. I'm reading too much into it. Too much into four words. It's more likely it was just a casual observation?

. . .

I think it was meant to invite inquiry.

. . .

You say, 'You forget, you know.' By 'you', you mean 'we'. Us. Human beings in general. And then you wait for me to say . . .

. . .

What do you forget?

SUSAN *looks at* MICHAEL *for the first time.*

So. What do you forget? Or we forget?

MICHAEL *stares back at* SUSAN.

MICHAEL. How difficult it is. To get children to go to sleep.

SUSAN. Oh.

SUSAN *starts working again.*

MICHAEL. She says she still has nightmares.

SUSAN. She does still have nightmares.

MICHAEL. Then surely –

SUSAN. It's only been a couple of weeks.

. . .

SUSAN *refers to her book, realises she has made a mistake.*

Damn.

. . .

SUSAN *looks up at* MICHAEL.

All children have nightmares. Everyone has nightmares. Don't you?

MICHAEL. You know I do.

SUSAN. Yes, but about that day?

. . .

I do.

MICHAEL. Do you?

SUSAN. You should.

MICHAEL. Nothing happened.

SUSAN. She could have died.

MICHAEL. She didn't.

SUSAN. We were lucky.

MICHAEL. I would have reached her.

SUSAN. I hope you would have.

MICHAEL. Naturally I think about it.

SUSAN. And naturally so does she.

. . .

Nightmares are expected. And healthy.

MICHAEL. What does she dream about?

SUSAN. Cold water. What do you think?

MICHAEL. I didn't know.

SUSAN. Did you ask?

MICHAEL. Do you ever ask what I dream about?

SUSAN. Your dreams are your own business these days, Michael.

. . .

MICHAEL. I miss her, you know, when I'm working.

. . .

SUSAN. Is it possible to miss someone you hardly know?

MICHAEL. She's my fucking daughter.

SUSAN. As if that makes a difference.

MICHAEL. What are you accusing me of, Susan?

SUSAN. Nothing. I'm not accusing you of anything.

Blackout.

Scene Four

MICHAEL, *alone.*

MICHAEL. They always ask me about the blood and guts. I always say, 'Didn't you see the photos?'

. . .

And then they say. 'Yeah. But what was it *really* like?'

. . .

MICHAEL *laughs to himself.*

Truthfully, I'm not sure. Read the papers.

. . .

It's *like* . . . it's not like anything. It's chaos. The most complicated and the simplest thing in the universe. The terrain changes, and the colour of the faces. But the bottom line is . . .

. . .

We want what you have. You have our land. We have your rights. We want your power. We don't want your God. Or your version of our God. You killed us, a year or a decade or five centuries ago. So now we'll kill you. And self-appointed witnesses will come to watch us do it.

. . .

There's a man I won't ever forget. I don't think of him often, but when I do I'm back there as clearly as I was the first time. On an unpaved desert road in the middle of a burning day, with green hills an unreachable promise on the horizon. He's sitting in the shade of a rock, at the end of a long groove in the ground, watching the sky. We were walking out of a village that had already been destroyed, cursing our luck because we'd arrived too late to see any action.

. . .

He barely turned towards us. Didn't get up to greet us as was customary in that part of the world. Seemed to have lost his enthusiasm. And his feet, which were lying at the side of the road about ten metres away.

. . .

We walked up to him. Three of us, all British, and a translator. I remember trying not to disturb the bloody grooves he'd left in the dust trying to escape from the sun. Not out of . . . well I was way beyond squeamishness by this time. I wanted to be able to get them in shot, pristine. I could see the headline. 'End of the road for..' Whoever. If I could just get a shot where the truncated, shattered ankles sticking out of his trouser legs weren't too obvious. Nothing too gory for the breakfast table.

. . .

I squatted down in the dust. I got my shots. He was sweating, grey. He'd shat himself. He had flies in his beard. He was dying.

. . .

It seemed to energise him. He said something to me. Looked right into my eyes. I didn't even look at the translator.

. . .

When you've been called a fucking bastard a certain number of times you recognise the phrase in any language.

Blackout.

Scene Five

MICHAEL *and* SUSAN*'s house.*

SUSAN *and* MICHAEL *are waiting for* SEAN *to arrive.* MICHAEL *is opening a bottle of wine. He pours two glasses and puts them on the table.*

MICHAEL. Is he a vegetarian?

SUSAN. No.

. . .

I phoned him to check.

. . .

Neither is he a religious fundamentalist, or a refugee, or a semi-psychotic member of an insurgent rightwing guerrilla army.

MICHAEL. Oh. Good.

SUSAN. So I can't imagine what you'll find to talk about.

MICHAEL. I am capable of normal conversation, you know.

. . .

When given the chance.

SUSAN. I know.

MICHAEL. So give me the chance.

SUSAN. I will.

MICHAEL. He'll be here soon.

. . .

You were right. About getting changed.

SUSAN. Oh?

MICHAEL. Yes. It seems . . . well you were right. There's a certain appropriateness to it.

SUSAN. We've invited a virtual stranger to our house, of course –

MICHAEL. That's what I mean. What I mean exactly.

MICHAEL *drinks.*

We're thanking him.

SUSAN. In a way, yes.

MICHAEL. We're showing our profound gratitude. For what he did.

SUSAN. If that's how you want to put it.

MICHAEL. For saving something precious. Like that story.

SUSAN. What story?

MICHAEL. It's French, I think. The story. Guy who wrote it had syphilis.

SUSAN. What the hell are you talking about?

MICHAEL. Just making conversation.

SUSAN. For God's sake, Michael. Can't you just –

. . .

Can't you just be normal for once?

MICHAEL. This is me.

SUSAN. I wish it wasn't.

. . .

Talking to you used to be a pleasure. I used to look forward to it. Now even when you're away, I dread the phone ringing. And when you're here –

. . .

SUSAN *laughs.*

Isn't that awful. I used to dread the phone ringing because it might mean you'd been killed. Now I just worry that I might have to talk to you.

. . .

MICHAEL. I'm surprised you want to be seen with me, even in your own home.

. . .

Half joking.

And in any case, this was your fucking idea. Just because the bloke dragged some kid –

SUSAN. Our kid.

MICHAEL. Out of a boating lake. Something any reasonably equipped human being would have been capable of –

. . .

Well except for non-swimmers –

SUSAN. Thank you.

MICHAEL. You feel you have to kill the fatted calf –

SUSAN. It's salmon –

MICHAEL. The fatted salmon. When we could have just sent him a cheque. Instead we have to spend a few hours uncomfortably trying to make conversation and telling him what a hero he is like a couple of teenage groupies.

. . .

I mean it'd be easier to have 'Thanks Sean whatever-your-name-is' just tattooed onto Alice's arse as a permanent reminder, wouldn't it?

SUSAN *is laughing.*

And stop laughing.

. . .

SUSAN *stops laughing. She looks at* MICHAEL.

SUSAN. You prick.

MICHAEL *and* SUSAN *look at each other. Long pause.*

MICHAEL. Sue, it's nothing.

. . .

Softly.

Nothing we can't fix.

A knock at the door.

SUSAN. He's here.

    SUSAN *leaves.* MICHAEL *pours wine into an empty glass.*

    SUSAN *re-enters with* SEAN.

    MICHAEL *turns, holding two glasses of wine. Small pause.*

MICHAEL. Sean!

    MICHAEL *walks over to* SEAN. *Realising that he can't shake* SEAN's *hand carrying two glasses, he hands a glass over.* SEAN *and* MICHAEL *now have a glass of wine each, but both have it in their handshaking hand. Both men swap their wine glasses to their other hand, and shake.*

MICHAEL. Take your coat off. You must be boiling.

SEAN. No . . . I'm alright. I mean . . . yes. I'll take my coat off . . . sorry . . .

    SEAN *starts to take his coat off, remembers he is holding a glass of wine.*

SUSAN. Oh. Here . . .

    SUSAN *takes the wine from* SEAN, *spilling a little on to his hand as she does so.*

    SEAN *appears to be having difficulty with his coat.*

MICHAEL. Oh for –

    SUSAN *looks warningly at* MICHAEL.

Here.

    MICHAEL *gives* SUSAN *his glass and moves behind* SEAN *to take his coat. For a moment it looks as if the two men are wrestling, but then* MICHAEL *takes the coat, and* SEAN *almost falls.*

Good God, you're soaking.

. . .

    SEAN *is standing, looking from* MICHAEL *to* SUSAN *and back again.*

SEAN. It's raining outside.

MICHAEL. I'll just hang this up.

> MICHAEL *leaves.* SEAN *absently licks wine from his fingers.*

SUSAN. Which glass is yours?

SEAN. I'm not sure, to tell you the truth.

> MICHAEL *enters, takes one of the glasses from* SUSAN.

MICHAEL. Come on, then, sit down.

> MICHAEL *leads the way to the table.*

> MICHAEL *and* SUSAN *sit at opposite ends,* SEAN *in the middle.*

. . .

Well. Cheers!

They clink glasses.

First obstacle successfully negotiated. The removal of the coat!

SEAN. Cheers.

. . .

Blackout.

Scene Six

Hotel room, London. As before.

MICHAEL, *onstage alone, smoking a cigarette and using another piece of writing paper as a makeshift ashtray. He is pulling on one of his shoes and lacing it. Another plane can be heard coming in to land.* MICHAEL *presses the rewind button on the tape recorder and listens back to a snatch of his own voice. He smiles to himself. As* TANYA *re-enters the room the smile disappears. She is dressed as before but without a jacket. The top two buttons of her shirt are also undone.*

TANYA. You'll fuck up the recording.

> MICHAEL *fast forwards to the end of the interview and switches the recorder off.*

MICHAEL. Never could resist the sound of my own voice.

> TANYA *laughs.* MICHAEL *looks at her for a moment.*

> Still can't resist you.

TANYA. You'd be surprised how many people can't.

> . . .

> Resist the sound of their own voices.

MICHAEL. Thank God. I was almost jealous for a second. And that sounded almost disillusioned.

TANYA. With what? With sitting in rooms like this one, week in, week out, while a succession of over-educated and over-valued culture monkeys try to out-cool each other for the weekend hangover market?

MICHAEL. They can't all be that bad.

> . . .

> Surely?

TANYA. If that's a subtle way of asking whether I'm sleeping with any of them, then no, I'm not. Because yes, they are all that bad.

MICHAEL. It wasn't.

TANYA. No. It wasn't, was it?

. . .

MICHAEL. So.

. . .

Shall we finish what we came here to do?

TANYA. I thought we had. One of us at least.

MICHAEL *(laughing)*. So now it's my fault you're unfulfilled?

TANYA *(irritated)*. Oh . . . fuck off.

. . .

MICHAEL. Look. I'm sorry.

. . .

I'm all yours.

MICHAEL *switches on the tape recorder and lies back on the bed, his head on the pillows.* TANYA *switches the tape recorder off.*

TANYA. What do I look like, your fucking analyst?

MICHAEL. Depends if I look like your fucking patient.

. . .

Actually, the only analyst I've ever had died of a heart attack about two weeks after I started seeing him.

. . .

TANYA *looks at* MICHAEL.

Don't look at me like that. It wasn't my bloody fault.

. . .

TANYA *softens.*

TANYA. Alright.

TANYA *switches the tape recorder on again.*

SCENE SIX 27

Your forthcoming exhibition is the biggest retrospective of your work yet mounted. How does that feel, as an artist?

MICHAEL *switches off the tape recorder.*

MICHAEL. Oh come on.

TANYA *looks quizzical.*

You can't play the fucking innocent with me, Tanya.

. . .

TANYA *switches the tape recorder on.*

TANYA. I really don't know what you're talking about.

MICHAEL. Then you're in the wrong job.

TANYA. It's a simple question.

MICHAEL. It's an open invitation to define myself as an artist.

TANYA. Well?

. . .

Aren't you?

MICHAEL. That doesn't matter. You're inviting me to claim I'm an artist.

TANYA. I don't see anything wrong in that.

. . .

I've always appreciated your work. On a very human level. Over the past few years especially. If you speak to something fundamental, human . . . doesn't that make you an artist, by definition?

MICHAEL. The point isn't what I'm seen as being. It's what I claim to be.

TANYA. So you claim you have no effect on others. Surely that's not for you to decide?

MICHAEL. No. What I don't claim to be is an artist, and I dislike the assumption that I'll define myself as such.

TANYA. It's just semantics.

MICHAEL. I've seen people disembowelled over semantics.

TANYA. You say potato –

MICHAEL. He say die like the dog you are, according to God's holy law.

TANYA. So photography isn't art?

MICHAEL. Oh grow up. This isn't the college debating society.

. . .

TANYA *looks at* MICHAEL, *shocked.*

Which I assume you were a leading light in.

. . .

What I –

. . .

MICHAEL *takes a deep breath, makes an effort.*

I couldn't give a toss. There. That's the reasoned and succinct answer to your question. Is photography art? I don't know and I couldn't give a flying fuck. Is poetry any use? Is a microwave meal cookery? Does anyone care?

. . .

TANYA. I had no idea I was on such thin ice. Conversationally.

MICHAEL. There is going to be an exhibition of my photographs.

TANYA. You wouldn't be here, otherwise.

MICHAEL. We wouldn't be *talking*, otherwise.

. . .

A look between them.

What I'm uncomfortable with is the assumption that the act of collecting my work together in a single room makes it art. Or me an artist.

. . .

Fuck the rest of them.

. . .

TANYA. And the reason for your evident discomfort is –

Another plane goes over. MICHAEL gets up from the bed and goes over to the window. He lights a cigarette. The noise of the plane fades away.

MICHAEL. Missed. Again.

MICHAEL smokes. He turns towards TANYA.

OK.

. . .

Holofernes and Judith.

. . .

TANYA. Holofernes?

MICHAEL. And Judith, yes. Very important, Judith. Without her Holofernes wouldn't be remotely famous.

TANYA. The bible?

MICHAEL. Well yes. In a roundabout way. He was an Assyrian General. She lived in a town he was besieging. She sneaked into his camp, softened him up with wine. And promises of sex and victory. Of course.

TANYA. Softened him up in every sense but the biological, I imagine.

MICHAEL. Very clever.

TANYA. And then?

MICHAEL. She cut his head off with a fucking big sword and displayed it on the city wall. Result, demoralised and leaderless Assyrian troops, victory for the besieged.

. . .

MICHAEL puts out his cigarette.

But that's all beside the point.

TANYA. Is it?

...

MICHAEL *stares at her, laughs.*

MICHAEL. For God's sake. This is not some half-arsed allegory. At least not as far as events in this room are concerned. And button up your bloody shirt.

MICHAEL *and* TANYA *are both laughing.*

MICHAEL *comes over to sit on the bed beside her.*

TANYA. Yes. I think I better had.

TANYA *fastens the top two buttons on her shirt and walks over to lean against the writing desk, leaving* MICHAEL *alone on the bed.*

MICHAEL *is about to start speaking again when* TANYA *cuts him off.*

Funny.

MICHAEL. I suppose so.

TANYA. No. I was in this room last week. (*Quickly, teasing.*) Oh don't worry, I wasn't having as much fun – just some dick of an actor who's released a record.

...

They've moved the furniture around.

...

TANYA *looks at* MICHAEL.

Haven't they?

MICHAEL *(defensive)*. How should I know? I've never been here before.

...

TANYA. Of course you haven't. Sorry.

TANYA *sits in the chair. Makes a point of paying almost childish attention.*

Anyway. Back to my bible story.

MICHAEL. Forget the bible. That's not important.

TANYA. Well, in terms of –

MICHAEL. In this context. The point isn't the story, but the painting.

. . .

There's a famous painting, quite a few actually, of this incident. Seventeenth century. The one I'm thinking of is by a woman called Artemisia Gentileschi.

TANYA. Which is spelled?

MICHAEL. Look it up.

TANYA *looks at him, hurt.*

Ar-te-mi-si-a Gen-til-es-chi.

. . .

Just how it sounds. I expect.

. . .

I don't know. But the painting itself was, is, one of the most gruesome images I've ever seen. Holofernes, on his back, a handmaid holding him down and Judith. Caught in the act of sawing through his neck.

MICHAEL *is caught up in his description.*

The sheets look soft. The blood is flowing down them in streams. It's amazing how the motion of the blood and the bodies is so well captured. The look of agony on his face, the determination on hers. The knowledge.

. . .

She's everything. Every wronged woman. Every town under siege from a power determined to destroy it. Every guerrilla fighter. At the same time. Symbolic of all these things and also simply what she is.

TANYA. A woman cutting a man's head off, right?

. . .

MICHAEL. Yes. But simultaneously everything else. The visceral and the symbolic don't come into conflict. But a photograph of mine –

TANYA. Which one?

. . .

For the sake of argument?

MICHAEL. It doesn't matter. They're all about death.

TANYA. 'Sarajevan shot in the head'?

MICHAEL. If you want. You know it?

TANYA. Of course I know it.

MICHAEL. I mean do you know it well?

TANYA. I've done my research.

MICHAEL. Don't doubt it. Describe it to me.

TANYA goes to the window, looks out of it, turns to MICHAEL.

TANYA. They'd never get you up here, you know. Too high up.

. . .

MICHAEL *stares at her.*

TANYA closes her eyes and keeps them closed throughout the next speech.

OK. A middle-aged man lying in the centre of the frame. Black and white. But black and white doesn't do it justice. His coat is black, jet black. What's left of his hair is white, but there are thousands of contrasting shades in between. It's more real than colour, somehow, isn't it? Behind him there's a wall. Wall of a block of flats with fucking great holes punched out of it by shellfire. There's a string of –

TANYA *laughs.*

There's a string of old women's . . . bloomers I suppose. Seems a bizarre word to use in the twenty-first century . . .

anyway . . . these bloomers are hanging out of a window
that's still intact. Holding the end of the string is . . .
I suppose she's the sometime occupant of the bloomers
in question. An old woman, looking down into the street.
The man's being held by a woman, young enough to be
his daughter –

MICHAEL. She *was* his daughter.

TANYA *(mild interest)*. Really? I didn't know that.

. . .

TANYA *has lost her train of thought. She opens her eyes.*

More matter of fact, as if she's playing a memory game.

Er . . . The young woman's got her . . . her left arm around
his.. her father's . . . body. Torso. Supporting him, while her
right hand is on his forehead. His face is slack. Like my
great-uncle after his stroke. But it's not a stroke because
under her right hand his forehead isn't there. And neither's
her right hand because it's kind of . . . submerged . . . in
this mess of . . .

. . .

Well. You know what that is.

MICHAEL. Yeah. It's obvious, isn't it? It was all over my
jacket. It's a good thing I had the lens cap on. When he got
shot. Or there wouldn't have been a photo at all.

. . .

That's the difference.

TANYA. The lens cap?

MICHAEL. No. Just that Artemisia Gentileschi didn't have to
wipe Holofernes's brains off her brush before she started
work. She wasn't attacked by a screaming, flailing Judith
for ghoulishly intruding on a moment of personal loss. She
had the long lenses of history and hindsight to work through.

TANYA. Assuming her subjects existed in the first place.

MICHAEL. Doesn't matter. They were in a place where they couldn't be touched and they couldn't touch her. All she came away with on her hands was paint.

. . .

I'm not comparing my work to her art. But I don't want that word putting into my mouth. Fuck symbolism. It's just that some of those people are still alive. In living colour. In pain.

TANYA. I see. So what about 'Dying teenage conscript, 1994'?

MICHAEL. What about it?

TANYA. Well, inferring from the title, that boy's dead.

MICHAEL. I know he is.

TANYA. And, art or not, that's one of the most beautifully composed photographs I've ever seen.

MICHAEL. Didn't even think about it.

. . .

I heard a shot, I turned a corner. The sun was going down on an East-West road. Behind him. He looked like a mound of earth. I heard him moaning. I shot a few frames off with the flash. I knelt down beside him and he'd died. There was nothing I could have done.

MICHAEL *seems genuinely haunted.*

The sunset behind him. His white skin. The fact he was staring directly into the camera. The sense of cold. It was fucking cold.

. . .

However that looks. Compositionally. It was a pure accident.

. . .

Accidental.

TANYA *goes to* MICHAEL, *holds his chin in her hands.*

She looks into his face and smiles.

TANYA. Composition. Accident.

TANYA *chuckles to herself.*

Do you really think anyone cares about the difference?

. . .

TANYA *is smiling.* MICHAEL *is not. They look at each other for a few seconds. Suddenly, the tape finishes and the tape recorder switches itself off with a loud click. They both look at it, startled.*

Blackout.

Scene Seven

MICHAEL *and* SUSAN*'s house.*

MICHAEL, SUSAN *and* SEAN *are sitting at the table. There is a large bowl of peanuts in the centre of the table, along with one empty and one half-full bottle of wine. A moment.* SEAN *takes a peanut and puts it in his mouth.*

SEAN. I'm sorry. I couldn't find an off licence.

SUSAN. That's fine, Sean.

SEAN. Just a petrol station. I know I should have bought wine –

SUSAN. Peanuts are fine.

. . .

SEAN. Well it was that, or coal.

. . .

I thought you'd probably have a gas fire or something.

. . .

It's rare, to have a coal fire these days. Just as I was getting here though I remembered a friend of mine who died. He developed an allergy to peanuts. Nobody knew. It just came on, like you can have a heart condition and play football every week until you suddenly keel over. But then I figured

. . .

Well. It's a million to one chance. Apparently.

. . .

MICHAEL. So, Sean.

. . .

SEAN. Yes?

MICHAEL. We never really got a chance to talk, the other week.

SEAN. No.

. . .

I mean there was no reason for you to . . . the ambulance and everything.

. . .

I just wanted to go home really. Get into some dry clothes. I didn't really see the need to hang around.

. . .

SEAN *takes another peanut.*

It was a surprise when you called. I didn't think . . . Well not that you wouldn't want to . . . But I didn't expect it –

. . .

Sorry. I don't mean I thought you'd be –

MICHAEL. Ungrateful?

SEAN. Yes. No.

. . .

I was only there for a walk.

. . .

I was surprised. People do that every day, but the papers . . .

. . .

Some bloke knocked on my door the next day. Wanted to take my photograph, but I wouldn't let him. Even when he said you were famous.

MICHAEL. Oh I'm not famous as such. Not really.

SEAN. Well I thought that 'cos I'd not heard of you. But he took it anyway.

. . .

I should have shut the door straight away, thinking about it. Cheeky bastard.

. . .

And then it was in the paper. Local man saves celebrated photographer's kid from drowning in lake. Except with fewer words. And a picture of me looking gormless.

SUSAN. That's how we found you. The paper gave us your address.

MICHAEL. There's no need to feel uncomfortable, Sean.

SUSAN. You did a good thing.

MICHAEL. A kind, unselfish act. That's all. We just wanted to say thanks.

SUSAN. A few drinks. That's all it is. Some dinner.

MICHAEL. It's . . . energising. To have visitors.

. . .

Isn't it, Sue?

SUSAN. Yes.

. . .

I work from home. In fact I don't see –

MICHAEL. I'm away quite frequently. For long periods. Overseas.

SEAN. I know. They told me what you did.

...

I don't read the papers.

...

It must be hard work.

MICHAEL. Well your arms tend to get tired if it's a very long article.

...

SEAN *looks at* MICHAEL.

SEAN. No. Your job. All those wars and that. Someone told me how many wars you'd been to.

...

I'd no idea there'd been that many.

...

Africa must be hard to get to.

MICHAEL. Well –

SEAN. And where you've just been. That other place.

...

Must be warmer than here, eh? Is that why you like it?

MICHAEL. Well I don't. As such. Like it, Sean.

...

It's something I ended up doing, and then I realised I could have an effect.

SEAN. I had one of your photos once and I didn't realise it.

SUSAN. In the paper?

SEAN. No. I don't read the paper. On a record sleeve, when I was a kid.

...

When I was a . . . I don't know, I reckon you'd say I was a punk, but I wasn't. When there were proper punks around I was just a toddler. I had spiky hair as well if you look at the pictures but I don't think I meant anything by it. But when I was about fifteen I heard this song on the radio. Dead noisy. I wrote the band name down on a bit of paper and kept it in my pocket. Then when I was in town I bought the record and the picture on the cover was of this . . .

. . .

SEAN *looks at* MICHAEL *and* SUSAN.

This little black kid, about eleven. With a gun. And he's pointing it at the camera and he's got no shoes on and that's not strange I guess, for an African, or it wouldn't be if he wasn't wearing a suit and tie. Like a really poor, small bank manager.

. . .

But violent.

. . .

And he's pointing the gun at the camera, like it's a toy. But it's real, probably, because you can see someone's legs on the road behind him. I mean the rest of them's there as well, but in the photo you can just see the legs. Dead legs. And you wonder. Well I wonder, you probably know. If the kid shot the guy who's dead on the road in the dust behind him. And if he's going to shoot the photographer. But that photo was by you, so I'm told, so I don't have to wonder about that now. Even if he did shoot you he obviously didn't kill you.

. . .

I can't remember what the album's called.

. . .

But that photo was by you.

MICHAEL. He didn't shoot me.

SEAN. Did he shoot –

MICHAEL. Yes.

SEAN. And what happened after –

MICHAEL. He got shot.

SEAN. When?

MICHAEL. About two minutes later. By some Government troops. Killed outright.

. . .

But I missed that.

SEAN. You'd already left?

MICHAEL. Oh no. I saw it.

. . .

I just couldn't change the film quick enough.

SEAN. 'The Business of War.'

MICHAEL *looks at* SEAN.

MICHAEL. Yes. That's an interesting way of putting it, Sean.

. . .

Simply the business of war. Just a chain of killings. Each one sparked off by the next. Each one a contribution to a momentum that's impossible to stop until ancient grievances have been avenged or all sides are exhausted by killing and counter killing. I like that. So matter of fact.

SEAN. No. 'The Business of War.' That was the name of the album.

. . .

It was crap, anyway.

. . .

Well I didn't like it. Maybe I should have listened to it more.

. . .

Did you know the band?

MICHAEL. It doesn't quite work like that. You see, when I got back to the hotel I sold the picture to a picture agency I had a contract with. A couple of years later they licensed it to the record company. The art department from the record company showed it to the band, and they all agreed it should be on the album cover. By that time I had nothing to do with it.

SEAN. Still. *(SEAN looks around him.)* At least you made some money.

. . .

What was the kid's name?

. . .

SUSAN *pours herself another glass of wine.*

MICHAEL. I don't know.

SUSAN. I wish you could have met Alice tonight, Sean, but she wasn't feeling well. She's in bed.

SEAN. That's OK. She probably wouldn't remember me. Kids forget stuff like that easily. Selective memories. She'll just remember going for a swim.

SUSAN. I think you're very modest, Sean.

SEAN. I know kids. That's all.

MICHAEL. Really?

SEAN. Yeah. Big family.

SUSAN. Well you'll know how much parents can worry. About their kids.

. . .

SEAN. Not really. Like I said. There was a lot of us.

. . .

SUSAN. Well what happened . . . what nearly happened to us, Sean.

. . .

You could say it would be every parent's worst nightmare.

SEAN. It's hard to keep an eye on kids. Especially outdoors.

MICHAEL. Well precisely.

SUSAN. Anything could . . .

. . .

Brightly.

Did I mention I've started taking swimming lessons.

SEAN. No.

SUSAN. You've inspired me to do that.

SEAN. I'm not a brilliant swimmer.

SUSAN. I. We. Michael and I. We want to thank you for saving Alice's life.

MICHAEL. I don't know what we would have done –

SUSAN. If anything –

MICHAEL. After a loss like that. I imagine it's difficult to –

SUSAN. You can't watch them all the time.

MICHAEL. No.

SUSAN. It's easy, with kids. To let them slip away.

. . .

I told her not to go near the water.

. . .

But do they listen? When she started to shout I couldn't work out at first. If she was playing, or . . . you don't know the fear.

MICHAEL. Nothing happened.

SUSAN. Is that the point?

SEAN. If I hadn't –

SUSAN. Exactly.

SUSAN *looks at* MICHAEL.

Exactly.

SEAN. No. If I hadn't, somebody else would have.

To MICHAEL.

You would have. I saw her first, is all. Did what you would have done if you'd seen her first.

MICHAEL. I could have saved her myself.

SEAN. But you hadn't seen her.

. . .

You hadn't seen her, had you?

MICHAEL. I was looking –

. . .

SUSAN *pours herself another glass of wine.*

Christ. We're getting through it, aren't we?

MICHAEL *makes as if to leave.*

I'll get some more.

SEAN. Not for me. It goes to my head.

MICHAEL. What? Big lad like you?

SEAN. I'm still not used to it.

MICHAEL. Still?

SEAN. It doesn't matter.

SUSAN. Get some wine, Michael.

MICHAEL *leaves.*

. . .

SEAN. There's no need for him to feel guilty.

SUSAN. Guilty?

. . .

No.

SEAN. I don't know why there was such a fuss. Everything's alright. It's not as if –

SUSAN. You're right.

SEAN. None of it really happened.

SUSAN. What d'you mean?

SEAN. Your Alice is upstairs, asleep. The only odd thing in this house is that I'm here.

. . .

I appreciate it. Dinner and that.

SUSAN. It's nothing.

SEAN. Seriously. I don't get out often.

SUSAN. No.

. . .

I know the feeling.

SEAN. Do you?

SUSAN. I'm not saying I feel –

SEAN. Trapped?

SUSAN. Oh God no.

. . .

I translate books. Into English. Technical manuals mainly.

SEAN. That's useful.

SUSAN. It's something to do.

. . .

It's something I can do at home. Any time of day. With Michael away so much . . . Well it's good to be able to work in the evenings.

SEAN. Yeah.

. . .

Don't you get bored, ever?

. . .

Blackout.

Scene Eight

MICHAEL, *alone.*

MICHAEL. The observer destroys the experiment. The photographer destroys the event. Light's a wave or a particle, depending on how you choose to look at it.

. . .

Are events unfolding because of me, or despite me?

. . .

Is it a coincidence that every time I raise my camera to my face the man next to me fires his gun?

. . .

Come with us, they said. In the early morning. They shook us awake in the cold. Come with us and we'll show you something. Good picture. Good picture. Last night we fought. Now we'll give you a good picture.

. . .

For us? You piled them up like that for us? How kind. How considerate. How proud your mothers will be.

. . .

Of course I'll give you a copy for your brother. He can put it on the mantelpiece. This is fucking crazy. Useful, but crazy.

. . .

They were killed how? In the fighting? Of course they were. And that's amazing aim on your part, isn't it? To have shot so many of them in the back of the head.

. . .

Of course I believe you. Of course I believe what you're doing is right. I'll say the same things to your enemies next week, but don't let that put you off. There can never be peace unless the land is yours. Your people earned it with blood, not these barbarian invaders. They've only been here five hundred years.

. . .

A transit camp? Of course it is!

. . .

The world needs to be told. The word needs to be illustrated. Particle, wave, wave particle. Humane treatment or execution? The world needs . . . the public needs . . .

. . .

This isn't science. Admittedly there are physical aspects but
. . .

. . .

Make me a channel of your bullshit. Make this shutter click catch the truth. What percentage of any given situation is constituted by one twenty-fifth of a second? What percentage of a war is constituted by a battle, of a freedom struggle, by one exploded school bus? One fucking nail bomb? How much do you think I can see?

. . .

From where I'm standing?

. . .

It's never my fight. I have never wanted to take up a gun.

. . .

Never.

Blackout.

Scene Nine

A bombed-out house, somewhere in the Balkans, 1994.

A battle is taking place outside.

MICHAEL *is making a call on a satellite phone.*

MICHAEL. I can't hear you . . .

> MICHAEL *changes position.*

Yeah. Got you now . . . I need some transport . . . no . . . I got some good shots but this is all fucked up . . . no, not *been* shot . . . yes, fucked up . . . I don't know . . .

> MICHAEL *moves urgently, looking outside.*

I'm about a kilometre outside the centre . . . on the road to . . . yeah. Heading west . . .

> MICHAEL *looks at his watch.*

About three hours . . . I don't fucking know. Near a church . . . Yeah the one with the bell tower . . .

> MICHAEL *moves urgently again, looking.*

Fuck. The one that had a bell tower until about twenty minutes ago . . . The what? . . . Who the fuck is Yu Wen? Is he fucking Japanese? What the fuck does he know?

. . .

> MICHAEL *listens intently.*

The fucking UN? . . . Fuck the UN . . .

> MICHAEL *listens for a longer period.*

Yes, well you see the problem with that is it's nearly dark and I don't fancy just running up to any cunt in a helmet . . . Yes I know they're fucking blue . . . Look out of the fucking window, Dave. What can you see? . . . Exactly . . . Yes I'm out of fucking cigarettes, what kind of a question is that? . . . Just get one of the drivers from the hotel down here . . . Well pay him fucking extra . . . Give him a bottle of fucking scotch then . . . Oh fuck off Dave, they'll do anything for booze . . . Dave? . . . Dave? . . .

MICHAEL *stares at the phone. He has been cut off.*

Oh shit.

MICHAEL *begins to redial.*

Blackout.

Scene Ten

MICHAEL *and* SUSAN*'s house.*

The peanuts have been replaced with the detritus of dinner. More wine. Music is playing in the background – something choral and classical, restful.

SUSAN. If you like, Sean, you could come down to London with us.

SEAN *and* MICHAEL *look up, surprised.*

Next week. Just for the day.

MICHAEL. I'm sure –

SEAN. Why?

SUSAN. There's an exhibition. Of Michael's photographs. We'd normally go on our own, and you know how these things are. These events.

SEAN. No.

SUSAN. Well they're . . . I think you'd find it interesting.

SEAN. Would I?

MICHAEL. I don't know about that.

SUSAN. Well they're always interesting for you, Michael.

. . .

You should see him, Sean. They all buzz around him like
flies round . . .

. . .

Like bees round honey. Editors, other photographers,
students. Journalists. I hardly get to speak to him all day.

. . .

You could come too. See what all the fuss is about.

SEAN. I don't read the papers.

MICHAEL. What do you do, Sean? Apart from accidental
heroics?

SEAN. I don't do anything.

MICHAEL. Well not necessarily . . . I wasn't referring to a job
as such.

SEAN. I walk.

MICHAEL. Where?

. . .

SEAN. I just walk.

. . .

SUSAN. Well, Sean, you don't have to read the papers.
Michael's photos speak for themselves.

SEAN. Worth a thousand words. I remember hearing that once.

MICHAEL. I'm not sure there's a precise value you can attach
to it, but Susan's got a point. In fact it'd be interesting to see
what somebody who doesn't read the papers . . . What the
impact of the image alone would be on someone operating
from a standpoint of . . .

. . .

Innocence isn't quite the word.

SEAN. Ignorance?

MICHAEL. That certainly isn't what I meant.

SEAN. Doesn't matter.

MICHAEL. I –

SEAN. Forget it.

SUSAN. It was just an idea.

MICHAEL. I wonder, Sean, that's all. Sometimes I'll be working . . . well if you can call it working.

. . .

The thought pops into my head and drowns out all the chaos that's going on around me. Does it mean anything, what I'm doing? Standing among the dead and the fighting and . . . the extremity of it all. Is it real?

. . .

That's all I meant. Does it . . . translate? Except into a powerful image for the front page?

. . .

Which is why I was interested.

SUSAN. All I thought was that it might be nice to have some company. You need company sometimes. Especially in London. It's a big place.

. . .

SEAN *looks at* SUSAN.

MICHAEL. I know what you thought.

SEAN. I can't come to London. I'm sorry. I've got plans.

. . .

I'm enjoying my dinner.

MICHAEL. I dodge fucking bullets, for Christ's sake. People die all around me.

SUSAN. Michael –

MICHAEL. And it makes you think, Sean. You make me think –

SEAN. All I did was jump into the water. It wasn't even that deep. She was just panicking because she couldn't see you. Kids are like that, always thinking situations are worse than they are.

MICHAEL. That I could stay here, you know? Build a huge fuck-off sound stage in the back garden. Hire extras and lights and make-up artists, and really go for it. If they want an image for the front page, something to catch the eye . . .

. . .

If it's that important. I mean they need this every day. There's a war on . . . there's always a war on somewhere.

SUSAN. Can't you just let it drop?

MICHAEL. Why trust something as important as the image of a war to the war itself? It's random and messy. You're never certain of getting what you want. But with research, careful preparation . . . God, the possibilities are limitless. War photography to order. We've got the story, now pose the picture.

. . .

Can I show you something, Sean?

. . .

Some photographs that you might not have seen?

SEAN. I don't know.

. . .

If you want to.

MICHAEL. Right. Right.

MICHAEL *gets up.*

I'll call you. When I'm ready, I'll call you.

MICHAEL *leaves. Blackout.*

Scene Eleven

MICHAEL, *alone.*

MICHAEL. There's a special way of looking that's only found in the nearly dead. I saw that boy alive. The first time I saw him alive he had that look. What there is in that look it's a . . . I don't know how to put this. A discontinuity. As if the shortness of time has robbed them of a sense of time. If a dying person looks at you . . . it seems they don't see . . .

. . .

No. Or rather, they do see. The shortness of time makes it non-linear.

. . .

Yes. Fuck yes. The dying see everything. When they look at you in those few short moments you're deprived of any means of hiding yourself. They see everything you ever did . . . I'm sure of that.

. . .

I turned the corner and discovered the boy in the road.

. . .

I might as well have been naked to him. He looked . . . betrayed. As if he'd opened his arms and God had spat in his face. That look of shock, you see it on the evil and the good but . . . you rarely capture it.

. . .

I took a picture. Then he was gone. That timeless look collapsing into a cold, cold space somewhere just out of his reach. Pain. Shock. Realisation. Gone.

. . .

Part of it went into me, I think. I'm . . . cold now. I'm always fucking cold.

Blackout.

Scene Twelve

A bombed-out house, somewhere in the Balkans, 1994.

MICHAEL *is sitting on the floor, making notes in a small notebook.*

MICHAEL. Killed 37 total . . . Two strategic villages in the enclave of . . . Massive movement of irregular troops to support . . . Vehicle destroyed by landmine . . . Headless child in road . . . Possible mortar attack on local market . . . Suspicion that attack deliberately set up by pro-government militia in order to . . . Battle for . . . Still raging after eight hours . . . Roads impassable . . . Coming winter . . . Prohibitive weather . . . Air strikes called off . . . Loss of historic bridge . . . Once beautiful tourist town . . . Teenage irregulars . . . Systematic rape and internment of . . . Evidence of widespread torture . . . Deliberate policy to withhold food aid . . . Rumours of possible hand over of power in . . . Alliances formed between . . . Shell hits hospital . . . Orphans widowed . . . Operation Confined to Barracks . . . Operation Back Turn . . . Peacekeepers stand by as . . . World has its eyes shut says . . . Refusal to look . . . Trapped behind enemy lines . . . Merry Fucking Christmas . . .

. . .

MICHAEL *rubs his eyes. Pulls a small bottle out of his pocket and drinks from it.*

He flips quickly through the notebook and laughs to himself.

They don't pay me enough for this.

MICHAEL *drinks again. Laughs. Blackout.*

Scene Thirteen

MICHAEL *and* SUSAN*'s house.*

SUSAN *and* SEAN *are alone at the table.* SUSAN *drains a glass of wine.*

SUSAN. Don't get married Sean.

SEAN. I won't.

SUSAN. It's like drowning.

. . .

It really is. Like being suspended in cold water and knowing that the next breath you take might kill you.

SEAN. It's difficult to get along with people. For a long time.

SUSAN. When I met him, he was fucking amazing, you know? Just like that, I was in love with him.

SEAN. I don't know what that feels like.

SUSAN. It's nothing special, after a while.

. . .

So we got married. Had a kid. Had this fantastic circle of friends. Action junkies. Filling the room with stories that they helped to tell, drinking too much, returning from all over the world with new scars and blazing eyes and . . . it was utterly amazing. The high when he walked through the door and I felt that he'd been out there pursuing something righteous. Making a difference.

SEAN. Doesn't he?

SUSAN. I thought so. To give him credit, he thought so at first.

. . .

Then at some point I realised that the only change was in him.

. . .

It's all the same, in the world. No such thing as cause and effect, you see. Only on a local level. It burns out in one place and it flares up in the next. Over and over again, and he goes to it and he takes his photos and he comes back and nothing changes. Except that every time he's a little more distant. And the stories stop being about the awfulness of it all and they start becoming about him. And the modesty becomes deliberate. And the charm becomes bullying, like a smell that overpowers everything else.

. . .

Drives the women crazy, you know. The ones that don't matter.

SEAN. I shouldn't be here. You don't know me and –

SUSAN. I'm glad you're here, Sean.

> SUSAN *pours* SEAN *a drink.*

Have some more wine.

SEAN. I –

SUSAN. It's alright. I'm not trying to –

> SUSAN *laughs.*

We make you uncomfortable, don't we?

SEAN. Yeah.

SUSAN. Don't be. We're just grateful. After all, if Alice had died it would have been the end. For us.

SEAN. He was watching, that day.

SUSAN. He hesitated. He can't forgive himself.

. . .

He's seen more dead children than anyone should.

. . .

It fucks you up when you have to try. To actually try, to care about the people you're supposed to love.

SEAN. He's very hard on himself. On you.

SUSAN. I know.

...

I just want to leave the bastard, now. And his fucking photographs. His dead babies and his dying soldiers. I want things uncomplicated. Black and white. You see a problem, you fix it. Find someone who does the right thing instead of illustrating the wrong.

SEAN. Leave him then.

SEAN *shakes his head.*

I shouldn't be drinking. I'm sorry. I didn't know I was going to say that.

...

I thought I was doing the right thing, once, and it got me into a fuck of a lot of trouble. It's not that simple. I just ignore stuff now. Try to live my life and not bother about what I can't see.

...

That's what fucks people up. Feeling like they have to see. Like they have to know. I don't want to know.

...

SUSAN. It said in the paper you were in prison.

SEAN. Yeah.

SUSAN. It didn't say why.

SEAN. Does it matter?

SUSAN. I shouldn't think so.

...

I'm sorry. I'm being too curious.

SEAN. It's OK. Nothing to tell really. Someone told me a friend of mine was fu –

...

– was having sex with my sister. She was fourteen. He was twenty-five. That's wrong. So I got pissed and went round to his house. I beat seven shades of shit out of him and put him in hospital for a couple of months.

. . .

Except it wasn't true. It was a wind-up. So he got his head kicked in and I got eighteen months. All on a rumour.

. . .

That's when I realised. You have to do the right thing, but only when you know what the right thing is. And unless it's happening in front of you, how can you ever know?

SUSAN. I understand.

SEAN. Thanks.

. . .

I know what it feels like. Drowning.

. . .

You just have to swim, in the end. Fuck the rest of them and swim.

Blackout.

Scene Fourteen

Hotel room, London.

TANYA *is sitting on the desk, making notes in a small notebook. She finishes her note and moves quickly to the tape recorder. She removes the tape from the tape recorder, writes on it, puts it into its box and pockets it. She puts in a fresh tape and hits the record button, returns to her sitting position on the desk.* MICHAEL *enters, drinking a glass of water, and settles himself on the bed again. He reaches for his cigarettes. The packet is empty. He screws it up and throws it in the waste basket.*

MICHAEL. You haven't got –

TANYA. No. Gave up.

MICHAEL. Why?

TANYA. Too expensive.

MICHAEL. I should probably get some more.

    MICHAEL *starts to get up.*

TANYA. We're nearly finished.

MICHAEL. Good.

. . .

    The interview. That it's nearly finished.

    TANYA *changes tack.*

TANYA. How much do you make? In a good year?

MICHAEL. Why?

TANYA. It's just a question.

MICHAEL. It's a loaded question.

TANYA. Interesting answer.

. . .

How loaded?

. . .

Would you say?

. . .

MICHAEL. Is this business or personal?

TANYA. I thought it was always personal to you.

. . .

MICHAEL *and* TANYA *examine each other.*

What do you want?

. . .

A fucking photograph?

MICHAEL. What for?

TANYA. Not worth it? Not enough pain?

MICHAEL. If you're trying to provoke me, I –

TANYA. Why would I be trying to do that? You're legendarily cool under pressure, after all.

. . .

Level headed enough to create some of the most enduring images of conflict in the last three decades. Not my words.

. . .

Cool enough to know when you've got your shot. To take the cheque and run.

. . .

Cool enough to watch your daughter drowning and wish you had a camera.

. . .

MICHAEL *gets up.*

MICHAEL. It's over Tanya.

TANYA. I think I've got enough.

MICHAEL *stops, turns.*

MICHAEL. Not just the fucking interview.

TANYA. I wasn't talking about the interview. And as for the fucking, well it never really got started. For me.

MICHAEL. Clever. Liked that about you from the first time we met.

TANYA. Yeah? I don't think I've ever felt this stupid.

TANYA *sits on the bed.* MICHAEL *is still standing.*

They are still speaking calmly, but clearly with restraint.

Because . . . do you know what you are?

. . .

No?

. . .

You're this week's weekend hard-on. Just another little boy, posing for the other kids in the playground, and pretending it was nothing. Look at me! I climbed the highest tree, and I nearly fell out. I jumped my bike over the wall. I played in the fire over and over and I never got burned. But it doesn't matter, because I can do it again. Because I don't care. Really. I impressed this woman into bed. I never got hurt, but I made some pretty pictures of some people who did and I'll let you see them if you give me some fucking pennies. They never shot at me because I never shot at them. I just let the big kids get on with killing each other and then I scooped up their guts and sold them to the world and I came home with sticky hands I can never quite get clean, but that's OK 'cos it was nothing. No really. I hurt my knee and I didn't even cry.

. . .

And do you want to be my friend?

. . .

MICHAEL. People die doing my job.

TANYA. People die catching fish for a living.

MICHAEL *smiles.*

MICHAEL. When you've had a single worthwhile experience, Tanya, give me a call.

MICHAEL *puts on his jacket, finds a fresh pack of cigarettes in his pocket, unwraps them. He takes one out, lights it. He throws* TANYA *the packet. She catches it.*

Then it might be worth my while taking your fucking picture.

They look at each other for a brief moment. MICHAEL *leaves.* TANYA *takes a cigarette from the packet and looks in her bag for a light. She doesn't have one. She lies back on the bed. A plane flies over.*

Blackout.

Scene Fifteen

MICHAEL *and* SUSAN*'s house. Another room.*

A table strewn with black and white photographs.

MICHAEL *is sorting them into piles.*

MICHAEL. I'm through here.

SEAN *enters.*

Come over here. I want you to look at some of these.

SEAN *walks over to the table and stands next to* MICHAEL.

SEAN. Why?

MICHAEL. I want you to understand what it is I do.

. . .

It's important. I want to know what you think.

SEAN. You know what people think.

MICHAEL. Not people. You.

SEAN *looks at the photographs but doesn't touch them.*

SEAN. I don't know any of these places.

. . .

I need to get another drink. Do you want another drink?

SEAN *starts to leave.*

MICHAEL. Hang on. You've done something for me. I want to do something for you. I want to explain.

SEAN. I don't need my eyes opening.

MICHAEL. I want you to understand.

SEAN. I know what you do.

MICHAEL *picks up a photograph.*

MICHAEL. It takes it out of you. To make a record like this.

MICHAEL *hands the photograph to* SEAN.

SEAN *looks at it, puts it back down on the table.*

Isn't it amazing, how you can tell it's blood, even in black and white? It looks sort of thick, doesn't it?

SEAN. You can tell it's blood because it's coming out of a person.

MICHAEL. But doesn't it speak to you?

SEAN. Yes. It says here's a woman on the ground with blood . . . buckets of it coming out of her. And she's got a massive hole in her chest.

SEAN *picks up another photo.*

And this one says here's a kid crying, covered in mud.

Another photo.

Here's a fat man in a uniform and a fur hat, laughing at an old thin man because he's making him dance. And this one says here's the old thin man again, on the ground, with his face in a puddle, which is a funny place to go to sleep.

. . .

But I guess he's not sleeping. And here's a starving woman with a starving baby, talking to a well-fed soldier. And here's a young bloke lying in the road in the night, looking at the camera and dying. And here's a big pile of kids. And here's a knife. And here's a man with a camera. Always.

. . .

SEAN *looks at* MICHAEL.

And here's a little girl, drowning. And there's the same man, watching, because he doesn't know what to do for a second. Whether to jump in and swim or take a fucking picture.

. . .

And here's a man with his entire life in a collection of flat dead people with no names to speak of, and a couple of nice plaques on the wall, and a family he doesn't even know.

. . .

It doesn't mean anything to me, this. I can't touch them. If I could touch them I could help them, and if I can't help them I don't want to see them.

SEAN *stacks the photographs neatly and turns them over.*

Who are you? I know what you are, but who are you, really?

. . .

How many kids have you watched, dying?

. . .

It can be an estimate. I don't expect you to remember them all.

MICHAEL. I don't owe you any sort of explanation, Sean. You did a good thing for me and my family, but this is none of your business.

SEAN. So why show me, then? So I can feel bad 'cos I can't do anything about it? Or do you want there to be a fucking revolution?

. . .

Peace on Earth and goodwill to all men? It doesn't work like that, though, does it? That's what you found out but you just keep on going and then you fuck up the things that maybe you can do something about.

MICHAEL. I choose to make sacrifices –

SEAN. You don't deserve to have the things you sacrifice.

. . .

I reckon . . . I reckon you were a good bloke once. So when did it all change?

. . .

You don't have to tell me. I'm just asking. I'm just some dumb fuck who never reads the paper. I don't make the news.

. . .

I acted on impulse, and I did a good thing. And your kid is asleep upstairs because I did a good thing. I did something that you couldn't do for a moment because you're not even sure what to do anymore. You can't do. You can only take.

MICHAEL. Information, Sean. If you don't have information –

SEAN. Where's the fucking information? Point one. People die sometimes. Point two. That's a shitty thing to happen. There is no point three.

. . .

You get one life. You live it. Anything else is bullshit.

MICHAEL. I want you to go now, Sean.

SEAN. You're just empty.

MICHAEL. You have my heartfelt appreciation.

SEAN. She deserves better,

MICHAEL. Just leave.

SEAN. Are all those wars worth it?

MICHAEL. Yes.

SEAN. No.

  SEAN *looks at the pile of photographs.*

  Just as dead as they are.

  Blackout.

Scene Sixteen

A bombed-out house, somewhere in the Balkans, 1994.

A VOICE *shouts unintelligibly offstage, repeating the same phrase over and over with increasing urgency. A gunshot.* MICHAEL *enters, walking backwards, taking pictures as he goes. Eventually he lowers his camera.*

MICHAEL. Thirty-eight.

  . . .

  MICHAEL *giggles.*

  He locates the phone and begins to dial.

  Blackout.

Scene Seventeen

Hotel room, London.

TANYA *is talking animatedly on a mobile telephone.*

TANYA. . . . No Joe . . . No . . . I'm fucking serious . . . Don't try to get around me, Joe, I know how fucking good I am . . . well you don't have to tell me . . . It was OK . . . I got enough stuff . . . that isn't the point . . . I don't want more high profile . . . No, Joe . . . a complete change, or nothing.

. . .

TANYA *listens. While she listens, she picks up the full cigarette packet, crushes it and throws it into the waste paper basket.*

Now you're talking . . . Where? Never fucking heard of it . . . I know it doesn't matter . . . There's always the internet, yeah . . .

How big? . . . Oh fuck off. A *small local insurrection*? I would have thought I'm worth . . .

. . .

Well, yeah. If you put it that way . . . these things can always get out of hand . . . when?

. . .

Fine by me. I'll file this fucker and get straight onto it . . . yeah.

TANYA *hangs up the telephone. She is smiling.*

Blackout.

Scene Eighteen

MICHAEL *and* SUSAN*'s house.*

SEAN *is wearing his coat, preparing to leave.*

MICHAEL *is sitting at the table.* SUSAN *is standing.*

SUSAN. It's late.

SEAN. There's a bus. Up the hill. I checked.

SUSAN. Stay the night.

MICHAEL. There's a bus. He checked.

SUSAN. It's just that it's late.

SEAN. I'm going to go.

SUSAN. Well I hope. I hope you've enjoyed yourself.

SEAN. It was nice meeting you both. I appreciate it. You didn't have to –

MICHAEL. Neither did you. But you did.

. . .

Thank you. For the peanuts.

SEAN. No problem.

. . .

SUSAN. I could run you home, if you'd like.

SEAN. You've been drinking.

SUSAN. Or call you a taxi.

SEAN. It's fine.

. . .

SEAN *smiles at her.*

I can look after myself.

. . .

You look after yourself.

. . .

Thanks for a good . . . for an evening.

SUSAN. Well maybe you can come again. It's always good to have visitors.

MICHAEL. What time's that bus?

SEAN. Ten minutes.

MICHAEL. You'd better –

SEAN. I will.

. . .

I hope she's alright.

SUSAN. She is. Thanks to you.

SEAN. Generally, though. I hope she's alright generally. It's hard to know what the best thing to do is when you've got to look after people.

SUSAN. You know what kids are like.

SEAN. I guess.

. . .

They have to work it out for themselves. Can't be there every minute, can you?

. . .

All you can do is leave them to it and hope for the best.

. . .

To MICHAEL.

Thanks for showing me your stuff . . . your work.

MICHAEL. It was nothing.

SEAN. I know. I'll look out for it.

SEAN *moves towards the door.*

Well. Maybe see you again.

SUSAN. I hope so.

SEAN. Maybe.

MICHAEL. Goodbye.

. . .

SEAN. Yeah. I'll let myself out.

> SEAN *leaves.* SUSAN *watches him go.* MICHAEL *drinks his wine.*
>
> *Blackout.*

Scene Nineteen

MICHAEL, *alone.*

MICHAEL. You're always asking yourself. 'How do you see this ending?' – By that I don't mean this particular firefight. This little spot of local difficulty, this minor revolution which is life and death for those involved and just another job for you.

. . .

You just mean . . . all of it.

. . .

What do I come back to? The coward's answer . . . the logical answer too is . . . I don't. Shoulder the guilt like a soldier's pack and keep on moving. When hope has been blown to shit and the world stops looking, keep on moving. When peace has reared its head for a while move on . . .

. . .

When you've exhausted all the options but honesty, keep on moving. Come home, but never for too long. Come back and sit in the old familiar chair surrounded by the old, unfamiliar people. Listen to the ticking of a kitchen clock and look at the strangers you've surrounded yourself with.

Only feel alive when you close your eyes.

. . .

Never, ever look in the bathroom mirror . . .

. . .

Be prepared if you do. For the honesty to come flooding in. Whatever it was I set out to do, I have failed, and now I do it as if waiting for a miracle. I know that miracle won't happen, but it's easier to pretend I believe.

. . .

I've done terrible things.

. . .

I've done nothing. About terrible things.

. . .

I might as well have been a blind man, for all the good I did. People died because of me. No. Well . . . people died in spite of me. Even after that became obvious I still . . .

. . .

I see it ending in fire. In a strange combination of inescapable gravity and brief weightlessness. Free fall. If I go back . . . one of these days, over a desert or a city or a worthless stinking piece of jungle, an engine will fail. A hydraulic system will blow, a missile will find the wrong target.

. . .

I always sit in the window seat. Insist on it whenever I can.

. . .

If there's time, I'll finish my drink. If there's time I'll unfasten my seatbelt.

. . .

Whatever happens, as the earth comes up to meet me, I'll be taking pictures. All the way down.

Blackout.

Scene Twenty

MICHAEL *and* SUSAN*'s house. The next day.*

MICHAEL *is sitting at the table drinking coffee and reading a paper.* SUSAN *enters.*

MICHAEL. I had a call. Earlier.

SUSAN. Oh.

MICHAEL. About the exhibition. Seems they want me to go down there a day early.

SUSAN. Really? Are you going to?

. . .

MICHAEL. I said I would. You don't have to.

SUSAN. No?

MICHAEL. Probably best if you just come down on the day.

SUSAN. Another interview?

MICHAEL. Just some photos.

. . .

SUSAN. I'm not coming.

   MICHAEL *looks up from the paper.*

   I thought I wouldn't.

MICHAEL. Would you mind telling me why not?

SUSAN. No reason really.

. . .

   Well I'm leaving you, but apart from that, nothing.

MICHAEL. I see.

SUSAN. Good.

MICHAEL. Where will you . . . where will you go?

SUSAN. I hadn't thought that far ahead, to tell you the truth.

. . .

I just know I'm going. Obviously with Alice.

SUSAN *leaves the room, returns with a pile of clothes, which she begins to fold.* MICHAEL *goes to stand next to her.*

MICHAEL. Let me –

SUSAN. Fuck off.

MICHAEL *sits again.* SUSAN *folds clothes as she speaks.*

You'll be leaving again soon, won't you?

MICHAEL. I imagine.

SUSAN. Where?

MICHAEL. There's a nasty little war on in the Middle East. I'm assuming they'll send me there.

SUSAN. That's not leaving, for you. It's being repatriated.

MICHAEL. Will you be here when I come back?

SUSAN. God no. We'll be long gone by then. Don't worry though. I'll tell you where we are. We're not just going to disappear. That would be unfair. Wouldn't it?

. . .

MICHAEL. Is there –

SUSAN. What the fuck do you think?

. . .

Of course not.

. . .

There will be. In time. I'm not completely on the shelf yet, am I? If I thought I'd used up all my chances on you, I'd end it all now.

MICHAEL. I don't –

. . .

MICHAEL *puts down the paper.*

I don't want you. To go.

SUSAN. You have no idea.

. . .

How little I care about that.

MICHAEL. I depend on you.

SUSAN. Is that what it's called?

MICHAEL. You're not being fair.

SUSAN. You are my husband Michael.

. . .

SUSAN *laughs.*

And I can't believe how fucking absurd that sounds.

. . .

It's not the infidelity, if that's what you're thinking.

MICHAEL. What –

SUSAN. Oh don't be fucking pathetic. It's the sheer bloody selfishness of it all.

. . .

This is a home. Not a foxhole. This isn't a place for you to wait until the next bit of reality kicks in. Until the next rush.

. . .

You appear like a fucking ghost and you're about as substantial. I never know what you're thinking and I don't think you do.

. . .

So I'm going to leave you to your awards and your dead boys and let you spend more time in the places you really love.

MICHAEL. I killed him.

SUSAN *looks at* MICHAEL.

That's why you're so important.

. . .

I stopped being human.

. . .

I love you.

. . .

The boy in the photograph ran towards me. I didn't know what I was doing. It was dark, chaos. You can't see a press badge in the dark. They should make them luminous, shouldn't they? There was a gun on the ground. Dropped. He ran towards me, shooting. I shouted. I shouted again. You can't hear bullets.

. . .

He wouldn't stop.

. . .

I'd never fired a gun before. It felt alive.

. . .

I shot him with the gun. And then. With the camera.

. . .

MICHAEL *looks at* SUSAN.

I'm sorry. About everything.

. . .

I don't want you to leave me.

They look at each other.

SUSAN *turns towards* MICHAEL.

He moves his hand towards her.

Blackout.

Scene Twenty-One

MICHAEL*'s photography studio, one year later.*

TANYA *is sitting in front of a plain white screen.* MICHAEL *is taking readings near her face using a lightmeter. There is a camera set up on a tripod with a remote switch attached to it by wire.* MICHAEL *returns to the camera, looks down into the viewfinder, makes adjustments.* TANYA *watches him.*

TANYA. I saw it. Your new exhibition.

MICHAEL. Show. It's called a show. Keep still.

TANYA. Exhibition. Show. Same difference.

MICHAEL. On the contrary. There's a very important difference. Exhibitions are for works of art. My show –

> MICHAEL *sets off a flashgun without any warning.* TANYA *winces.*

Is merely an interesting set of things for people to look at if they choose.

TANYA. It's very moving.

> She. Alice. She's very . . .

> Beautiful. Vital.

> And he looks so calm. Strong. Wherever you put him. In whatever setting. The calm at the eye of the storm.

> Did it surprise you? That he became a friend.

> MICHAEL *straightens up and stares at* TANYA.

MICHAEL. Old habits die hard, don't they?

TANYA. Meaning?

MICHAEL. This isn't an interview. I'm no longer your subject matter. You're mine.

> . . .

> And no. I wouldn't call him a friend.

TANYA. What would you call him, then?

MICHAEL. A personal fucking affront. At first. Then a challenge. Then a presence.

Like a –

TANYA. Ghost?

MICHAEL. Fuck no. He's far more solid than that. Just a part of the landscape. Like a tree or a park bench.

TANYA. Or a lake?

MICHAEL. No. He isn't dangerous. He's just there because he happened. Happens. To be there. He isn't going to go away and in some respects he's the reason she's still here. So why not photograph them together?

TANYA. I like them. They're good pictures.

MICHAEL. They're simple pictures of a simple subject. What's not to like?

TANYA. And did they help? Do they?

MICHAEL. They're selling. They're the reason I get more commissions. Like this one. Simple pictures. Book jackets. Trees. Things not even a shot-to-shit action man can fuck up.

TANYA. You know I didn't mean that.

MICHAEL. In that case nothing helps. It isn't a therapeutic process. It's just a process of. Undertaking. Other projects. While I forget. Lose the taste in my mouth.

TANYA. I'm rather getting used to the taste.

MICHAEL. You wouldn't be here if you weren't.

. . .

Your book's good. Insightful.

TANYA. You read it.

MICHAEL. Not all of it.

TANYA. Brought the taste back?

MICHAEL. Like sour fucking bile.

. . .

Accept that. It'll turn for you. Spoil.

TANYA. I don't –

MICHAEL. I'm not trying to put you off. Just watch for the warning signs. And get out when you see them. Don't ignore them.

TANYA. Like you did.

MICHAEL. I lost everything. It's still not all come back. Not yet.

TANYA. Do you miss –

MICHAEL. Do you want to fuck me for old time's sake?

TANYA. No.

MICHAEL. Good.

. . .

TANYA. It's the best decision I ever made.

MICHAEL. Thanks.

TANYA. No. The job.

. . .

I suppose you pushed me into it. Accidentally.

MICHAEL. In that case I should be apologising.

TANYA. Not at all. I travel. I talk to interesting people and folks who are trying to kill interesting people. I've sipped brandy with sweaty warlords in clapboard shacks in the forest. I've watched executions and exposed the killers to the world. I've seen bombs change the shape of desert mountains. I've fucked in cheap hotels with mortar rounds landing in the street outside. And I've made a difference. I've saved lives and shortened wars that nobody had previously even known were going on.

. . .

It's a good life.

MICHAEL. You keep telling yourself that.

. . .

You need to. You need to believe in the power of truth, and in the truth of what you show. Even if the belief itself is bullshit.

TANYA. That's what you did?

MICHAEL. That's what I stopped being good at. And then. I was fucked.

The camera flashes again. MICHAEL *seems satisfied.*

That's you done. Or at least a reproducible version of you.

TANYA. So what now?

MICHAEL. A week away. North. Hills against the sunset. Empty lakes at dawn. Coffee table shit.

. . .

I can feel it changing me. I might even be starting to like it.

. . .

And you?

TANYA. Something always comes up.

MICHAEL. With or without you. Either way. Remember that.

There is a moment of silence. MICHAEL *smiles slightly.*

MICHAEL. And don't go getting killed.

. . .

It makes it harder to go on living. Afterwards.

Silence. Blackout. Ends.

A Nick Hern Book

Safety first published in 2002 as an original paperback
by Nick Hern Books Limited, 14 Larden Road, London W3 7ST,
in association with Unlimited Theatre, Leeds

Safety copyright © 2002 Chris Thorpe

Chris Thorpe has asserted his right to be identified as
the author of this work

Front cover photograph: Danielle Senior

Typeset by Country Setting, Kingsdown, Kent CT14 8ES
Printed and bound by Bookmarque, Croydon, Surrey

A CIP catalogue record for this book is available from
the British Library

ISBN 1 85459 711 6

CAUTION All rights whatsoever in this play are strictly
reserved. Requests to reproduce the text in whole or in part should
be addressed to the publisher.

Amateur Performing Rights Applications for performance,
including readings and excerpts, by amateurs should be addressed
to the Performing Rights Manager, Nick Hern Books, 14 Larden
Road, London W3 7ST, *fax* +44 (020) 8735 0250, *e-mail*
info@nickhernbooks.demon.co.uk, except as follows:

Australia Dominie Drama, 8 Cross Street, Brookvale 2100,
fax (2) 9905 5209, *e-mail* dominie@dominie.com.au

New Zealand Play Bureau, PO Box 420, New Plymouth,
fax (6) 753 2150, *e-mail* play.bureau.nz@xtra.co.nz

United States of America and Canada Unlimited Theatre
(see below)

Professional Performing Rights Applications for performance
by professionals in any medium and in any language throughout
the world (and by amateurs in the United States of America and
Canada) should be addressed to Unlimited Theatre, Aire Street
Workshops, Studio 11, 30-34 Aire Street, Leeds, LS1 4HT,
fax +44 (0113) 234 5400

No performance of any kind may be given unless a licence has
been obtained. Applications should be made before rehearsals
begin. Publication of this play does not necessarily indicate its
availability for amateur performance.